FROM HERE TO ETERNITY:

PREPARING FOR THE NEXT ADVENTURE

BRUCE EPPERLY

Energion Publications
Gonzalez, FL
2016

ISBN10: 1-63199-226-0
ISBN13: 978-1-63199-226-1

Energion Publications
P. O. Box 841
Gonzalez, FL 32560

energion.co
pubs@energion.com

DEDICATED TO THE MEMORY OF
MY MOTHER-IN-LAW MAXINE GOULD
MY PARENTS EVERETT AND LORETTA EPPERLY
AND MY BROTHER BILL EPPERLY.

TABLE OF CONTENTS

CHAPTER ONE
IN THE MIDST OF LIFE

For everything there is a season,
and a time for every matter under heaven:
a time to be born, and a time to die. (Ecclesiastes 3:1–2)

One midweek morning, Susan called me at my study and requested that I stop by to see her on my way home that afternoon. Susan and her husband of forty years Phil were among the saints of my church. In the year that I'd been her pastor, I had companioned with her on cancer's roller coaster ride. For a while the treatments appeared to be working, but now they had reached an impasse with no certain remedy in sight. The most recent regimen had left Susan so physically weak and mentally fuzzy that she could no longer do what gave her great pleasure, painting, writing poetry, and taking walks with Phil. Tests confirmed that chemotherapy could no longer keep her cancer at bay. The cancer had spread throughout her body. She could enter an experimental protocol, but there was no guarantee of success and there was also the likelihood of serious side effects.

Around the kitchen table they had shared for four decades, Susan told me of their decision to forgo any further treatment. "We had hoped to get a few more years. We'd even hoped for a cure. We wanted to travel and spend time with our grandchildren. But, now we're opting for quality, not quantity. I want to live well until I die, playing with my grandchildren, finishing a few canvasses, and leaving a legacy of poems for my children and Phil. We've prayed about this, and now it's the time to let go."

As a pastor, I believe such conversations are sacred. They are "thin places," as the Celtic Christians say, where divinity and humanity meet. I took a few breaths to spiritually center, and then inquired as I've done many times in similar situations, "How are things with your spirit?" Susan and Phil looked lovingly at one another as she responded, "I know what this means. I'm going to die, but I know that I'm in God's hands. I know that death isn't the end.

I've lived a good life, done good work, and loved my family, friends, and church. I hate to give all this up, but I know God won't let me down." Three months later Susan died, leaving a legacy of love and a life well-lived. Her memorial service on Thanksgiving weekend was truly a celebration of life and affirmation that Love is eternal.

The Reality of Death. "In the midst of life, we are surrounded by death," so wrote Protestant Reformer Martin Luther. In life there are no guarantees nor can we insure the safety of our loved ones and ourselves. Even among healthy and young persons, a car accident, heart attack, stroke, or diagnosis of an untreatable illness can come with no warning and when we least expect it.

The story is told of a servant who encountered Death at the bazaar in Bagdad. Frightened by his encounter, he raced home to his master. "Please let me have your fastest horse," he begged. "I just saw Death at the marketplace and I'm going to flee to Samarra. He won't find me there." Being a kind man, the master lent his horse to his servant and sent him off with a blessing. Being a bold man, he confronted Death in the bazaar and challenged the Grim Reaper. "Why did you frighten my servant?" he demanded. Somewhat taken aback, Death responded, "I didn't mean to scare him. I was simply startled to see him. You see, I have an appointment with him this evening on the road to Samarra."

The mortality rate remains 100% despite our technological advances. Still, there is something about the human spirit that defies death. Deep down we have a sense of immortality and can't imagine the reality of our non-existence. Diagnosed with terminal cancer, author William Saroyan quipped, "Everybody has got to die, but I always believed an exception would be made in my case. Now what?"

I know how Saroyan felt. Now in my sixth decade, I can no longer claim to be in midlife, as many baby boomers do, unless I make it to 125! Yet, on certain days, I feel sixteen or twenty-five and when I'm playing baseball or rough housing with my young grandchildren, walking on the Cape Cod beach down the road from my church, working on a writing project, or taking a few minutes for meditation, I feel eternity in the midst of time. There is a spark in us, something holy and divine, which participates in everlasting life. There is something dynamic and timeless that shines regardless of our age or physical condition. We experience ourselves as being part of an adventure that is bigger than our lifetimes and lures us toward new horizons.

Still, everything hinges on the "now what?" that perplexed William Saroyan. Once we recognize that life — and let's get personal, "my life" and "your life" — is finite, we need to ask ourselves "What are we going to do with this unique and precious life that has been given us?" Once we truly realize that we don't have forever, at least, in this lifetime, will we live in fear or savor each moment, including the most painful and challenging ones? Will we greet each fleeting day with worry or with the affirmation, "this is the day that God has made and I will rejoice and be glad in it?" (Psalm 118:24).

The Psalmist asks God to make our mortality meaningful. "Teach us to count our days that we may gain a wise heart" (Psalm 90:12). As a friend asserted, after he was diagnosed with incurable cancer, "I don't have time to mess around. I'm not going to let anything get in the way of living. I'm going to greet each sunrise with joy and each sunset with gratitude." "Each day matters," noted a 95-year-old widower I encountered at a Hyannis, Massachusetts, coffee house. "When I was younger, I thought I had forever. I thought my wife would live forever and that she'd be with me at the bedside. But, she didn't make it. I was with her when she went. I want to make to one hundred but that's just a few more years. I have no illusions. I'm going to die and pretty soon. Even if I stay healthy, I only have a handful of Christmases left and what if dementia sets in. I know how brief my stay will be. Now, each day is a cause for celebration."

Our human adventure can be described in the counsel of the Hasidic Rabbi, Simcha Bunim (1767–1827):

> Everyone must have two pockets, with a note in each pocket, so that he or she can reach into the one or the other, depending on the need. When feeling lowly and depressed, discouraged or disconsolate, one should reach into the right pocket, and, there, find the words: "For my sake was the world created." But when feeling high and mighty one should reach

into the left pocket, and find the words: "I am but dust and ashes."

We are heavenly dust, sparks of the divine that must eventually be extinguished, at least in this world, and that is the source of our greatest joy and most abject sorrow. Our mortality is inevitable, and an abundant and joyful life involves accepting the reality of death. But, our deaths are not entirely natural phenomena, without anxiety or care. Our deaths are not always like the gentle fall of an autumn leaf, especially if our dying process involves certain types of debilitating physical or mental diseases. Once we reach a certain age, we experience the reality of death not as abstraction, but as a concrete reality. We realize that eventually everything we love will be taken from us and that we will be taken away from this world, perhaps entombed in a cemetery, stored in an urn, or scattered along the seashore.

Even young children have momentary glimpses of mortality. Recently, my four-year-old grandson told me, "When you die, Grandpa, I'm going to marry Grandma." Young children rehearse the reality of death, first, in their observations of the natural world and, then, in contests between sharks and whales and heroes and villains, in which one dies and the other lives on. It may take a few more years for the child to internalize that the fact that he or she will die as well, but death is our constant companion from the moment of conception.

We are dust, but we reach to the heavens in imagination, creativity, wonder, and sacrifice. In that contrast between spirit and flesh, imagination and concreteness, and life and death, we experience the greatest joy and creativity as well as the greatest fear and grief.

Pause a moment, take a deep breath, and say out loud, "I am going to die." How does it feel to admit your mortality? What images come to mind? When I used a variation on this exercise at the study upon which this book is based, participants responded with:

- I'm excited to find out what's next.
- I feel anxious.
- I'm not afraid of death, but of the dying process, the pain, and losing my sense of control.

4

- I have trouble believing I will die.
- What will happen next?
- I'm hopeful about the future.
- I feel a sense of loss. I don't want to leave my family and friends.

Even people who are confident about the afterlife as a result of near death experiences or deep faith in God have moments of anxiety and uncertainty about what's next in our human adventure.

Death as the Doorway to Spiritual Transformation. The encounter with death can lead to denial or transformation, emotional shutdown or spiritual open-heartedness. We can flee to Samarra, acting as if we can escape death, only to ride into the hands of our greatest fears. We can also embrace the reality of death and discover that each moment is a miracle. According to a Buddhist legend, young Gautama was a wealthy Indian prince. Early his life, his father received a prophecy that his son Gautama would be a great spiritual teacher. Desiring that his son follow in his footsteps as a political and military leader, he tried to shield him from all of life's difficulties. He surrounded him with youthful companions, servants, and dancing girls, who were discharged as soon as wrinkles appeared. But, one day, Gautama escaped the palace and wandered about the city. In the course of his meanderings, he encountered something that he had never experienced before — an elderly man. Puzzled by the realities of aging, he returned to the city and on two successive days, he encountered a sick person and then a corpse. Troubled, Gautama ventured forth one more time, and beheld a monk. From then on, he recognized that all things must pass, and that we can experience peace only through embracing change, letting go of attachments, and deepening our spiritual lives. Out of Gautama's encounter with death, one of the world's great wisdom traditions was born. He became the Buddha, the "enlightened one," whose teachings have inspired millions to face the challenges of death with equanimity.

Resurrection Living. Two grief-stricken women trudged to the graveyard to pay their last respects to their beloved friend and teacher. "Who will roll the stone away from the tomb?" they asked one another. To them, death had sealed their future and the fate of their beloved friend and teacher. When they arrive at the tomb, the stone is rolled away and the tomb is empty. They are amazed and awestruck, but know that the One they loved is alive and will meet them on the path ahead (Mark 16:1–8).

In another Easter story, one of the women, Mary of Magdala, cries out to a gardener, "Where have you taken my beloved friend?" (John 20:11–18). Her spirit soars when the gardener calls her name, "Mary." Her beloved companion lives. Love is stronger than death.

"In the midst of death," Martin Luther also asserts, "we are surrounded by life." That first Easter, the power of death was unmasked. Yes, pain is real and loss is devastating; but there is something more. New life springs forth. The crocus emerges after the chill of winter. The butterfly bursts forth from the tomb-like chrysalis. This is resurrection living. This is the pathway we take, mortal and finite, which leads beyond the grave and takes us from here to eternity.

CHAPTER TWO
A GRIEF EXPERIENCED

> But we do not want you to be uninformed, brothers and
> sisters, about those who have died, so that you may not grieve
> as others do who have no hope. For since we believe that Jesus
> died and rose again, even so, through Jesus, God will bring
> with him those who have died. (I Thessalonians 4:13–14)

Three weeks following her spouse's death, Deborah reported
that "The day Diane died I looked up in the sky and one star
shined brighter than usual. That was her shining self, shimmering
in God's grace, I thought. Nowadays, I see Diane whenever I look
at the sunlight shining through the trees or whenever I hear some
of our favorite music — Judy Collins, the Beatles, Joni Mitchell.
Sometimes I start tearing up; other times, I rejoice that we had a
decade together."

Just as death is universal, so is grief. In the wake of his wife Joy's
death, C.S. Lewis notes, "bereavement is a universal and integral
part of our experience of love. It follows marriage as normally as
marriage follows courtship and as autumn follows summer."

Grief joins celebration and loss. Grief reflects the intimacy and
importance of our relationships to persons, companion animals,
and prized objects. Grief tears apart the fabric of our lives, leaving
us emotionally, spiritually, and physically bereft and vulnerable.
Grief leaves us emotionally shattered. It can sever our ties with
others and eclipse our hopes for the future. The experience of grief
can also open us to experiencing the wonder of life, the importance
of relationships, and the trustworthiness of God. Grief can deepen
our faith and compassion for others who struggle with loss.

In responding to the grief experiences of his fellow followers
of Jesus, the apostle Paul counsels "we do not want you to be unin-
formed, brothers and sisters, about those who have died, so that you
may not grieve as others do who have no hope" (I Thessalonians
4:13). For the apostle, grief is appropriate at the loss of beloved
friends. He and the communities he pastored had lost scores of

friends and family through persecution, natural causes, and accidents. Paul's own life was in danger. Still, the apostle recognized that the healing of grief emerges when we discover that our lives and the lives of our beloved companions are in God's hands and that "nothing can separate us from the love of God in Christ Jesus our Lord" (Romans 8:38–39).

Grief is an essential component in the perpetual perishing of life. The emergence of each new moment requires the loss of its predecessor. Novelty and innovation involve letting go of even the best moments of the past. The river of life eventually takes everything we love from us, including our closest human and animal companions.

An encounter of a grieving woman with Gautama Buddha, the great wisdom teacher, captures the universality of loss in a world of change. A distraught woman comes to Gautama, asking the Enlightened One to revive her recently deceased child. Buddha recognizes her pain and tells her that a healing will occur if she can bring back a few mustard seeds from the nearest village. There's a catch to the Enlightened One's counsel, however. These mustard seeds must come from a home where no grandparent, parent, child, sibling, or beloved animal has died. The grieving mother ventures forth in hope, but returns later that day, having experienced an unexpected healing — the realization that all things, including our loved ones, must pass and that wholeness comes as the result of embracing and then letting go of our losses.

Still, the loss of beloved friends and family can be emotionally overwhelming. In describing his reactions to the death of his wife Joy, C.S. Lewis confesses, "I had my miseries, not hers; she had hers, not mine. The end of hers would be the coming of age of mine." When a close friend or family member dies, we may commit her or his future to God's everlasting care. Our lives, however, must go on without her or his touch, voice, and companionship. Our hearts are wounded, and in those first weeks and months following our loss, we wonder if we will ever be the same again. The truth is that we won't! But, the One who received our loved one in death is also our companion in life. This is the meaning of the theological term, omnipresence: God is with us in every moment and life situation.

Whether we rise in joy or descend in grief, God is our everlasting companion, and even in our grief, God has plans for us, "for good and not for evil, for a future and a hope" (Jeremiah 29:11).

A Pilgrimage through Grief. Grief involves a kaleidoscope of experiences, rather than clear and uniform stages. The experience of grief is ambient rather than linear. Grief touches every aspect of our lives. Like a physical wound, its impact is multifaceted and shapes our spirit, body, mind, and relationships. Over time our sense of loss is transformed yet never fully goes away. Although it has been several years, I still vividly recall finding my brother's lifeless body in the mobile home we purchased for him in Lancaster, Pennsylvania. I still go over our relationship, lamenting missed opportunities to be more supportive of him in facing the challenges of mental illness and loneliness. I had been a supportive brother, yet I still experience a sense of guilt at sins of omission that might — although in reality probably wouldn't — have made a difference in his quality of life. There are days that I miss my parents, and wish we could have one more phone conversation and visit.

Grief is personal and intimate like our relationship to God. When Jesus calls Mary's name on Easter morning, he is reaching out to her uniquely and intimately out of all the people in the world. He is speaking her name and addressing her grief in the only way she can understand. In like manner, our own unique life experiences shape our grief and God's healing touch in our lives. Still, we need guides for grief and one of the most insightful accounts of grief comes from the pen of C.S. Lewis. Lewis' classic account of his response to the death of his wife Joy Davidman, *A Grief Observed*, provides a pathway to finding healing in the midst of our own losses. Twenty years earlier, Lewis attempted to provide a solution to the problem of evil in *The Problem of Pain*. With the death of his wife, Lewis' academic and armchair theology was tried in the crucible in his own grief. Concrete pain trumped academic orthodoxy as he attempted to find God in the midst of grief.

In the aftermath of his wife's death, Lewis confesses that Joy's "absence is like the sky, spread over everything." He feels listless and lazy. He wants company but wants to be left alone. His body cries out for her touch and he worries that some idealized experience of Joy will replace the truly human, fallible person with whom he loved. Life has lost its luster and has become a process of waiting, not sure of what's going to happen next, and wondering if the long valley of grief will ever give way to a horizon of hope.

Grief, Lewis notes, involves a series of thwarted impulses that shape the texture of our relationships. "Thought after thought, feeling after feeling, had H. for their object. Now their target is gone." Over the course of Jerry's sister Julie's long journey with cancer, they called or e-mailed one another nearly every day. Knowing that Julie wasn't a morning person, typically, he called her every evening after supper. They shared pictures of their lives, vignettes from their families, and reports of her physical condition and treatment plan. Jerry flew cross country to visit Julie every other month. One evening, he called and no one answered. Panicked he called her son, who informed him that Julie had fallen into a coma. Jerry caught the next plane to the West coast to be with her for the final days of her life. Nearly a year has passed and Jerry still thinks of her each evening and reaches for the phone after supper to give her a call. Like Jesus' first followers Jerry has had to come to terms with the reality that she is no longer here and out of his reach, at least for now. When we met for coffee following the year anniversary of Julie's death, Jerry confessed, "I miss her so. She was my little sister and I was her protector when we were children. But, I couldn't protect her from cancer. I know we will meet again in heaven, but today I wish I could tell her how much I loved her and hug her once more."

After my mother unexpectedly died in 1990 from a pulmonary embolism following surgery, I continued the "old school" ritual of calling my father on Sunday evenings when the long distance rates were lowest. Each time we talked I felt the urge to ask my Dad, "Let me talk to Mom." Our relationships are made up of rituals. Along with the loss of touch and voice of our beloved companions, thwarted rituals fill us with a great sense of loss.

Our experiences of grief are physiological, emotional, tactile, and relational. They are inherent in nature and not just reserved to humankind. Studies indicate that dolphins, monkeys, horses, dogs, cats, and elephants experience the pain of separation from beloved animal and human companions. Wherever there is attachment and wherever there is love, there eventually will be grief.

Grief is a spiritual issue as well. The loss of a loved one calls into question, for many people, including C.S. Lewis, their previously held images of God. What seemed certain — doctrines we affirmed without question — now is challenged. In the course of our questioning, some images of God may die, after having been discovered to be inadequate or too superficial to respond to our experiences of grief or worse yet, abusive in minimizing our experiences of suffering. A champion of orthodoxy, Lewis now has to experience the divine absence which calls his previous beliefs into question.

> Meanwhile, where is God? This is one of the most disquieting symptoms. When you are happy, so happy that you have no sense of needing Him, so happy that you are tempted to feel his claims upon you as an interruption, if you remember yourself and turn to him with gratitude or praise, you will be — or so it feels — welcomed with open arms. But go to Him when your need is desperate, when all other help is vain, and what do you find? A door slammed in your face…. Why is He so present a commander in our time of prosperity and so very absent a help in time of trouble?

Lewis asserts that he still believes in God. Belief in God is part of his spiritual DNA. "The real danger," Lewis confesses," is of coming to believe such dreadful things about God." He worries that the God of love may be eclipsed by the cosmic sadist, who hurts us only to help us, and disregards our individual pain in light of God's quest for the greater good.

Healing Grief. There is no recipe for transforming grief to gratitude. In fact, the quest for a uniform antidote to the pain we experience may be a form of spiritual or emotional objectification. Like the pain that comes as the result of a broken bone or an operation, the healing of grief has its own personal timetable. Some call Goodwill or the Salvation Army to pick up a deceased spouse's clothing within a few weeks; others need to wait for a few years. Some get on with their lives and form new relationships quickly; others are more deliberate and eventually learn to savor their lives as widows or widowers. They know they will never meet anyone to replace their beloved and learn to embrace the beauties of life without a marriage partner. God's call to wholeness is always personal and shaped by our values, experiences, and hopes. It is important to honor our own grief and the grief of others.

As friends of those who have lost loved ones, we need to open our hearts to their pain without judgment or expectation. Our greatest gift is our willingness to be present in ways that are most helpful to the ongoing well-being of our friends. We need to reach out, and also let them guide the texture of our relationship. We need to be open to laughter, tears, and feelings of relief as well as depression. If questions of faith become important, we need to remember the importance of listening without judgment or the need to defend God from their expressions of doubt, disbelief, or anger. Job's friends were helpful in their silent companionship. It was only when they tried to set Job right theologically did his friends bring new pain into Job's life. God is often less orthodox and more flexible than our theological certainties. We need to trust that God is at work equally in our doubt and anger as well as our certainties and faithfulness. Our friend's questioning of God may indeed be a divine work, a process of divine midwifery in which needed images of God may be born.

Still, our experiences of grief never go away nor should they. We don't want to forget our beloved and our memories will always be bittersweet, as life itself always is, filled with gratitude and love, and also touched by pain and loss. Still, we can be sustained by the biblical promise that love never ends and that God has a vision for us and our beloved aimed at good and not evil, a future and hope.

CHAPTER THREE
ADVENTURES IN THE AFTERLIFE

"Look," Stephen said, "I see the heavens opened up and
the Son of Man standing at the right hand of God." (Acts 7:56)

Cheryl was in her early twenties when she encountered God
"on the other side." Raised in a nominally Roman Catholic family
in a Boston suburb, she checked out of religion entirely by high
school. The 60's lifestyle of rock bands, folk music, and parties
provided all the religious fervor she needed until her car went off
the road on a trip to Connecticut. In the blink of an eye, she
found herself catapulted into another world. She felt herself in the
company of an Indescribable Love whom she identified as Jesus.
Enveloped in light she knew that everything would be alright and
that her life was in God's hands. "Jesus was like a big brother,
looking out for me, protecting me and making sure I'd be safe.
I felt complete acceptance even when Jesus showed me where I
was hurting myself and others. There was no judgment or threat,
just a question, 'Is this the person you want to be?' I was at peace
and could have stayed with him forever, but knew I needed to go
home when pictures of my parents and little sister flashed before
my eyes." Now fifty years later, Cheryl's life is still defined by the
images of that evening. She entered a helping profession and, recently retired, she now volunteers at the local hospice. Although
she has the normal anxieties of aging baby boomers, she is certain
that she is God's hands, and death will be the entry way into life
everlasting with Jesus as her companion.

Christian theology, at its best, has lived between the poles of
certainty and humility. On the one hand, we trust our experiences
of God's presence in our lives and shape our behavior by our theological descriptions of God's nature and work in the world. On
the other hand, we recognize that no word or experience can fully
describe God and that every image of God, even those that most
deeply shape our faith, is finite, relative, and shaped by our own

imperfections. We can talk about God, but God is always more real than any words can say. As Zen Buddhists assert, we should not confuse the moon with the finger pointing at the moon or reality with our descriptions of it. This same counsel applies to near death experiences. They are real and life-changing to those who have them. Yet, they are also beyond everyday language, pointing to something we can't fully grasp. Moreover, our deepest experiences are always shaped by our particular culture, religion, and personality type. As William Blake says of mystical experiences — and near death experiences are mystical in nature — "if the doors of perception were cleansed, everything would appear to [humans] as it is, infinite." Alas, we are finite, and only God has an infinite perspective. Still, reports of near death experiences, like mystical experiences, reveal deeper dimensions of reality than the five senses can provide and open the door to a wider universe in which death is a transition to an even more abundant life.

The Witness of Near Death Experiences. Personal accounts of near death experiences reflect our time of emerging cultural and spiritual transformation. In the 1950's heyday of North American institutional religion, most people went to church but seldom talked about spirituality in public. Today, church attendance has declined significantly, but people are more open about their spiritual experiences. According to a Pew Research Center study, nearly half of North Americans claim to have had religious or mystical experiences compared to 22% in 1962. While the proliferation of mystical experiences may be due to a unique outpouring of divine inspiration, I suspect that the increase in reporting of encounters with the holy is the result of an interplay of our current religious pluralism, openness to spiritual practices, and the growing number of persons who claim to be on spiritual pilgrimages that take them beyond the rationalist philosophies and orthodox religious traditions that characterize the modern world.

In many ways the acceptance of near death experiences as religious in nature parallels the growing interest and research in the role of spiritual practices in health and healing. Both point to realities beyond technology, rationality, and orthodoxy. They invite us to a new "enlightenment" in which people seek to experience the spiritual energy and mystical amazement that gave birth to the world's great religious traditions.

Cheryl's near death experience is an example of the phenomenon of passing to the "other side" and returning to this world. While each near death experience is as unique as the persons who have them, there are certain common characteristics of near death experiences.

1) A sense of floating above your physical body and transcending the limitations of physical existence.

2) Observing people around you, often trying to bring you back to life and hearing medical professionals comment on your condition.

3) Going down a tunnel, often connected with hearing a buzzing noise. Persons report being drawn or pulled beyond physical life to another dimension. The passageway to the next dimension is often described in ways similar to the birth canal. Dying we are born again in a higher spiritual dimension.

4) Encountering friends and relations, and other spiritual beings. On occasion, these encounters involve persons of whose death the person having a NDE was unaware.

5) Encountering a Being of Light, whose characteristics are described as all-knowing and all-loving, and who is often identified as Jesus by Christians.

6) Life review, in which one experiences her or his whole life in panoramic form. The review is experienced as an opportunity for reflection and self-awareness, not punitive judgment.

7) The decision to return, often involving questions such as "Do you have unfinished business?" or "Is your earthly life complete?"

8) Ambivalence about coming back to earth, often provoked by the beauty and peace that is characteristic of the world beyond.

9) The return, usually involving awareness of coming back to the body, or observation of people providing medical resuscitation.

15

10) Inability to fully describe what happened in the other spiritual dimension. Like most mystical experiences, near death experiences take us beyond everyday experience and our typical language sets. One has difficulty finding the right words, if any words are possible, to describe one's experience of the world beyond. Persons often feel ambivalence about sharing what they have experienced. They fear that they will be misunderstood or labeled as eccentric or even worse. Our recent openness to spirituality and mysticism has given people greater courage in sharing their experiences. In a study group on life after death I led at South Congregational Church, three members felt comfortable sharing about their own near death experiences.

11) A sense of peace regarding death. Like many other types of mystical experience, near death experiences are life transforming. People report less anxiety about death. They know that a beautiful future lies ahead of them. Although the dying process may be difficult, they now know there is nothing to fear about death itself. Often persons come to appreciate the wonders of this life and become more mindful in their relationships, choosing to live in the present moment rather than always planning for a faraway future.

Although there have been attempts to explain near death experiences in terms of physiology, pharmacology, neurology, psychology, and hallucinations, these mystical experiences remain life-transforming to those who have them. Parallel scientific explanations may not discredit the reality of near death experiences. In a holistic universe, mind, body, and spirit are interconnected. What shapes the spirit shapes the body, and what shapes the body shapes the spirit.

This-worldly Encounters with Everlasting Life. Can the dead communicate with us? Is there a "thin place" in our relationships where the "living" and "dead" meet and where our deceased friends and relatives communicate with us? Do our thoughts and prayers somehow pierce the veil between this life and the next?

These questions are also unanswerable and subject to a variety of perspectives.

For example, until recently, many Roman Catholics believed in the doctrine of purgatory, an intermediate state of purification for persons eventually destined for a heavenly reward. The doctrine of purgatory depended on affirming the interdependence of this world and the next. At its worst, the doctrine of purgatory encouraged monetary contributions to reduce the time of purification for ourselves and others and a false reliance on our ability to save ourselves and those we loved apart from God's grace. Martin Luther's objection to the selling of indulgences was central to the Reformation. He was incensed by the marketing of the afterlife, characterized by Tetzel's jingle, "A coin in the coffer rings, a soul from purgatory springs." Still, despite Luther's objections, prayers for the dead were grounded in our desire that loved ones experience a reduction in punishment and a speedy entry into God's complete presence. The doctrine of purgatory describes a world in which the living and dead are in relationship: while we may not "know" what the dead are doing, we can influence their quality of life by acts of love and sacrifice on their behalf.

Many people believe that the dead are able to communicate with us, either directly or indirectly. My mother loved bright red cardinals and commented joyfully whenever she saw one perched in one of our backyard trees. Following her death, I found myself noticing cardinals wherever I went. Was this a result of my being more attentive or did they reflect my mother's desire to communicate with me?

Following her mother's death, Gloria had a dream in which her mother apologized for not being emotionally present throughout her life. Her mother shared about her episodes of depression and anxiety, much of which she had hidden from Gloria. She told her daughter that now she was at peace and that her daughter need not fear her own depression. Her message to Gloria was "remember, God is with you, as he is with me now. I wish I'd known this when I was raising you."

More dramatic are encounters in which a deceased relative appears to contact a child or parent. Seamus recalls waking up in the middle of the night feeling that he was not alone. His father's unexpected death from a heart attack left Seamus heartbroken. Though he and his father were close, he wished he had the opportunity to say "goodbye" and tell his dad "I love you." He yearned to hear his father's voice and feel his warm embrace. As he rubbed his eyes, he saw his father sitting at the foot of his bed and looking lovingly at him. Then he heard words that healed his broken heart. "Son, I love you. I wish we had more time, but I loved you more than anything in the world and when you have your own children I'll love them, too! Wherever you are, I'll be by your side." Seamus now has his own children and often invokes his father's wisdom and love to help him in his own parenting. Seamus is grateful for that moment when time and eternity met. "I now know that love is eternal and that I can call on my dad whenever I feel lost."

To the rational, analytic mind, such experiences are nonsense or forms of wish-fulfillment. But, these holy moments come from a place beyond our rational control or understanding. We may not be able to understand these experiences, but they change our lives forever, restoring our spirits, and giving us hope for the future. They tell us that God is love and love is eternal.

CHAPTER FOUR
IMAGES OF THE AFTERLIFE

"Truly I tell you, today you will be with me in paradise."
(Luke 23:43)

Just a few days before his death, Theresa asked her husband if his death was near. He responded affirmatively, and added "Hallelujah, I'm ready to meet Jesus." During his three-year journey with cancer, he had been sustained by faith in the resurrection of Jesus. Theresa remembers Phil saying on his last Easter: "I dream of the day when Jesus will call my name just as he did with Mary of Magdalene in the garden."

A few days before my mother-in-law's death, my wife Kate asked her, "Are you afraid of dying?" She shook her head "no." Kate continued, "Are you looking forward to seeing your family in heaven?" To which she smiled as she nodded with a "yes." Many of us are sustained in life's difficult moments — the death of spouse or child, debilitating illness, and our own death — by the faith embodied in one of my mother's favorite hymns, sung at her own funeral:

When peace, like a river, attendeth my way,
When sorrows like sea billows roll;
Whatever my lot, Thou hast taught me to say,
It is well, it is well with my soul.

These are not "pie in the sky, when we die" sentiments. In fact, for many persons, the hope of survival after death inspires a commitment to bring justice and beauty to this earth. The promise of immortality eases the pain of dying, but for them it is not an "opiate," as Karl Marx suggested, deadening their empathy with others. They have come to realize that in this wonderful life, every day matters and that we are also creating the contours of everlasting life for ourselves and others by our ethical commitments in this lifetime. Our acts of kindness and quest for justice bring beauty to this earth and provide a foundation for life eternal. They believe that if your neighbor has an eternal spirit, then he or she deserves respect and honor in this lifetime.

Symbols of Immortality. Psychiatrist Robert Jay Lifton affirmed the importance of symbols of immortality. Lifton believed these images give us meaning and hope and enable us to respond to the fleeting nature of life. According to Lifton, five symbols inspire and undergird our sense of life's meaning:

1) *Biological immortality* — living on in our children, grandchildren and beyond. This was the promise God made to Abraham and Sarah: you are mortal but your children will as many as the sands of the sea.

2) *Creative immortality* — the positive impact of our lives, most especially our vocations (work, art, literature, parenting) on those who will outlive us. The belief that our influence will endure and have a positive impact on the lives of others after we have died.

3) *Natural immortality* — our sense of connectedness with the universe beyond ourselves. Our experience of being part of larger planetary story from which we have emerged and to which we will return. Psalm 8 captures the spirit of natural immortality: "When I look at your heavens, the work of your fingers, the moon and stars that you established, what are human beings that you are mindful of them, mortals that you care for them? Yet, you have made them a little lower than God, and crowned them with glory and honor."

4) *Theological* — the belief that the spirit continues beyond the grave. Death is not the end but an invitation to further adventures and spiritual evolution. As the apostle Paul affirms, in light of the resurrection, "Death has been swallowed up in victory. Where, O death, is your victory? Where, O death, is your sting?" (1 Corinthians 15:54–55).

5) *Experiential Transcendence* — mystical experiences that connect us with higher dimensions. The sense of immortality emerging from encounters with the holy and near death experiences. In such moments, the doors of perception are opened and we experience the infinite realities underlying everyday reality.

The great wisdom traditions recognize each of these symbols of immortality. The great religions emerge from a sense of the sacredness of life, see birth as an opportunity for growth and new life, inspire ethical activity for the good of others, affirm that importance of embodiment in the spiritual journey, and anticipate further adventures beyond the grave. The various religious traditions express the holiness of the human adventure and imagine the afterlife in different ways. Still, healthy spirituality, regardless of our faith perspective, trusts in eternity, while affirming the importance of this lifetime.

Describing the Afterlife. Recently one of our church's children made the following affirmation, "When people die, they come back. But, bad people don't come back, or get any Christmas presents." Out of the mouth of children can come great wisdom. At the heart of our visions of the afterlife is the belief that there is "something more," that death is not the end, and that in one way or another we "come back," either to another lifetime or continue a heavenly journey in companionship with God.

The great world religions assert two contrasting visions of the afterlife. The wisdom traditions of the West — Judaism, Christianity, and Islam — typically affirm that we have only one earthly life and that our life continues in another realm beyond the grave. The wisdom traditions of the East — most especially, Hinduism and Buddhism — see our lifetime as one of many incarnations, the nature of which is dependent on our moral behavior and spiritual insight. The vision of the afterlife in terms of many incarnations, or reincarnation, has become essential to the world view of the many new age or new spiritual movements. In what follows, we will go on a brief afterlife adventure, pointing out the main points of the visions of heaven and hell and reincarnation.

Heaven's My Destination. I grew up in revival Christianity. The central element of our faith was getting right with God so that when we died, we would be with God and experience the joys heaven, and conversely escape the flames of hell. I recall many an altar call, our Baptist way of describing the invitation to accept Christ as your savior, being prefaced with "Today, if you had a car accident on your way home, where would you be going to, heaven or hell?" This was pretty frightening stuff for a small child and I was determined to go to heaven and experience eternal life. The alternative seemed far worse than any punishment my parents might mete out to me.

Years later, I heard a televangelist make the following statement, "If you got into a rocket ship and flew far outside our solar system, you would eventually find a place called heaven." For him, heaven was a physical place, geographically located, somewhere above the earth's atmosphere. Although he didn't go into the location of hell, I suspect he understood this place of terror in ways that the ancients did, physically or spiritually below us and eternally distant from God's heavenly bliss. Today, few people chart the location of heaven physically or assume that you could find heaven with some sort of supernatural GPS or online mapping system. Still, many people affirm heaven as their ultimate destination. They believe that nothing can separate us from the love of God, not even death, and that the saints will "fly away" from the ambiguities and pain of this earthly life.

Contrary to some people's beliefs, there is no consensus among Christians about our heavenly destination or frankly the criteria for passage through the pearly gates. Some believe all will eventually find a home with God; others see a strict separation of saved and unsaved, and heaven and hell-bound humanity. Still others affirm an intermediate state, purgatory, a place of cleansing and purification for those persons whose eventual destination is God's heavenly realm. Today, many Christians have come to believe that we will be reunited with our companion animals in heaven. The One who loved the lilies of the field and the birds of the air surely has a home for all our beloved non-human friends. They believe that if God loves the world, everything God loves will be preserved in God's memory and quite possibly in God's everlasting realm of Shalom.

It may come as a surprise to many Christians that resurrection, not heaven, was the primary image of hope among Jesus' first followers. Christian faith is Easter faith. On Good Friday, all hope is lost among Jesus' followers when their beloved teacher was crucified. His male disciples abandon him and the savior dies in agony and humiliation. On Easter morning, women come to the tomb to anoint Jesus' body and worry that they will be unable to roll away the stone that seals his tomb. To their amazement, the tomb is empty and angelic messengers proclaim that Christ is risen and is going ahead of them. In the various, and sometimes contrasting resurrection stories, the Risen Jesus passes through walls, appears and vanishes, enters conversations, breaks bread, breathes new life, cooks, and shares in a meal. He is alive and gives life to those who follow him. The One whose sacrifice liberates us from sin is victorious over all the powers of death.

No one quite knows what happened on Easter. It is beyond the limits of rationality and yet it gave birth to the Christian movement. Christ's resurrection gave courage to the fearful and hope to the lost. The resurrection can never be reduced to physiology or metaphor. Literal descriptions can't capture the wondrous mystery of life emerging from death. Nor can wish-fulfillment or hallucinatory experiences explain the courage and spiritual authority that emerged among those who abandoned Jesus in his hour of deepest need. Resurrection is always more than we can imagine, and resurrection was the hope of the first Christians. They imagined an ultimate transformation in which body, mind, spirit, and relationships would share in Jesus' resurrection life. The resurrection they hoped for inspired them to go out into the world proclaiming forgiveness, new life, and healing.

Resurrection is holistic and communal. The spiritual body of which the apostle Paul speaks in 1 Corinthians 15 is more rather than less than our earthly lives. We live in hope of being part of God's everlasting life in a community of praise, healing, and love. While resurrection hope was never fully described in the early Christian movement, it enabled both former persecutors and the persecuted faithful to believe that in life and death nothing can separate us from the love of God in Christ Jesus our Lord (Romans 8:39).

In the centuries to come, images of heaven and hell displaced the original hope of resurrection. Faithful believers lived in hope of the beatific vision of God awaiting them at the hour of death. Heaven was the destination of those who trusted Jesus and accepted God's grace in life and death. No one was ever fully able to describe heaven either. We hear of images of pearly gates, great reunions, and eternal praise. When I asked members of my "From Here to Eternity" class about their hopes for heaven, I received the following responses:

- Heaven is a place of eternal peace and joy.
- I look forward to meeting my loved ones and being reunited with them.
- I think heaven is simply union with God.
- Life will be beautiful.
- It will be eternal love.

However described, heaven represents our hope for complete healing and spiritual fulfillment. What is unfinished and incomplete here will be completed. What is painful here will be healed. Whatever is alienating here will be restored. The ever-present God whom we experience only partially now will be known to us as fully and lovingly. Heaven means that love, both human and divine, never ends.

But, if heaven is love and beauty, what is hell? Again, there is no consensus among Christians about the nature or reality of hell. When I was a child, I thought like a child, as the apostle Paul says. I saw hell as a place of darkness, punishment, and loneliness. Hell was being lost and unable to find your way home. Hell is, according to traditionalists, the absolute absence of God for those who have turned their backs on God's ways in this lifetime. Unlike the traditional Roman Catholic doctrine of purgatory, the temporary place of cleansing and purification for those whose eventual destination is heaven, hell is eternal imprisonment with no possibility of parole. It is the place of pain, punishment, darkness, and (ironically) fire and brimstone.

The doctrine of eternal hell has been morally and spiritually problematic to many Christians for a variety of reasons:

- The punishment doesn't fit the crime. Hell involves an infinite punishment for finite misbehavior and disbelief.
- Human decisions in relationship to God or others are seldom isolated and individual. Our behavior and ability to believe is influenced by factors such as family of origin,

place of birth, mental health issues, and parents' religious attitudes.

- Hell represents an ultimate defeat to God. God is either not powerful or loving enough to rescue the perishing.
- The doctrine of predestination, which in its traditional form asserts that God chooses both the saved and damned, portrays God as unconcerned about the well-being of creation and solely motivated by power. This vision of God is unworthy of Jesus' sacrificial love. You can fear, but not love such a deity.
- The criteria for "going to hell" are uncertain: is salvation a matter of divine choice, following rituals, participating in the sacraments, accepting Jesus as your savior, or good behavior? Who gets a "pass" on eternal punishment — children who have not reached a certain age, persons with mental illness or intellectual disabilities, or "holy" persons who have never heard of Jesus? Having accepted Christ, can we lose our salvation? Or, is it true that "once saved always saved?"

The unwarranted torture of hell has led some to believe that while heaven may not be their destiny, the unsaved and unrepentant will have their spirits eventually extinguished. They will miss the joys of heaven, but also be delivered from eternal punishment for finite actions.

Throughout history, many Christians have suggested a theological and spiritual alternative to the dualism of heaven and hell. They assert that when the scriptures proclaim that God is love, they really mean it. They also believe that Jesus' love for outsiders suggests that no one is ultimately outside of God's circle of love. For them the role of preaching and evangelism is to help people know how much God loves them and how they can experience healing and transformation by saying "yes" to God's unconditional grace. Our actions and beliefs have consequences, but God's love is greater than our sin, and God has the love and patience to lure every prodigal child home.

This viewpoint, indeed my own viewpoint, is that God guides and loves us from conception to death and beyond, and that beyond death, we are in God's hands. Our personality survives and we must deal with our sins and imperfections, and our alienation and failure, in the afterlife but that our healing comes in an environment that is completely supportive of our deepest desire to be in companionship with God. Salvation is universal, and also evolutionary. We grow in grace and holiness in a realm where we review our lives, make amends in a safe environment, and discover fully the wonders of ourselves and others. We will see ourselves and our calling fully, fully understanding God's vision for our lives, as Paul suggests in 1 Corinthians 13. Heaven is not a static place but a place of constant growth and adventure. We still have vocations beyond the grave and while I can only speculate here, I believe that our vocations involve infusing greater love and joy into the worlds for which we are responsible. Heaven's our destination but the destination is the open door to experience "more than we can ask or imagine."

Many Lives Ahead of Us? Recently, as I was waiting in line at a local coffee house, I overheard a conversation between two women in which one described a series of unfortunate events. She concluded her description with the words, "I must have some really bad karma. I wonder if some past life mischief is catching up with me!" All of us want to make sense of the unexpected and seemingly meaningless events of life. Is good or bad fortune arbitrary? Does it come from a mysterious but omnipotent power? Or, do we somehow bring these apparently chance events upon ourselves by our previous actions?

There are times when it is clear that we reap what we sow. In his song, "Cat's in the Cradle," the late singer-songwriter Harry Chapin describes a father's lament that his son had become just like himself, too engrossed in work to have time to reach to him. Lack of exercise and a diet saturated in fat and processed foods may eventuate in heart disease. Negativity can lead to the absence of friends in one's senior years.

A major stream of biblical thought contends that good fortune is the result of righteousness while sickness and poverty reflect sinful behaviors. Jesus was once asked if a man's sight impairment was the result of his or parents' sinful actions. While Jesus like Job challenged linear understandings of reward and punishment, morality depends on the connection between actions and outcomes for us and others. Grace abounds but it must work within the context of the impact of human personal and institutional decisions.

One of greatest mysteries of life is the apparent arbitrariness of our births. We come into life in families, with health conditions, economic backgrounds, cultures, genders, ethnicities, and religious traditions that expand or contract our ability to live joyfully and abundantly. I thank God daily for the gifts of my birth in an education-oriented, middle-class North American family. At first glance, I have to ask myself "Is my birth entirely accidental, God's will, a combination of chance and providence, or the result of the impact of a past life?"

The apostle Paul once said "the wages of sin is death" (Romans 6:23). The doctrine of reincarnation asserts that "the wages of ignorance is rebirth." Reincarnation, the belief that this lifetime is part of stream of lifetimes, is essential to Hindu and Buddhist philosophy. It is also a significant element in the syncretic philosophies of nineteenth and twentieth century theosophists and members of today's new spiritual or new age movements.

Simply put, reincarnation asserts that our births are the result of the impact or energy of previous lifetimes. We have all lived before and our start in life is far from accidental or divinely-determined. In fact, it is an exact reflection of who and what we were in a past life. Our current lifetime or incarnation is but one of many, perhaps even thousands, of previous lifetimes, each of which has an impact on my current existence. The goal of life is self-awareness which liberates us from rebirth. The problem of life is that our ignorance and sense of individuality and isolation blinds us to our true divine nature. We are one with God, but fixate on the temporary aspects of life as if they are eternal. We confuse the soul with body, just as in daily life we often focus on clothes, status, and reputation rather than the enduring realities of life.

The doctrine of reincarnation asserts that we go from life to life until we learn the spiritual lessons that will free us from any further incarnations. According to Hindu spirituality, our destiny is to return the One Eternal Reality, Brahman, just as the waters of

Ganges River flow to the sea. Beneath the changing seasons of our lives and our many lifetimes is the enduring, blissful self, Atman, identical to the Universal Soul, Brahman.

Although Buddhists typically deny the existence of an eternal, unchanging soul, they believe that liberation from rebirth comes by letting go, or becoming unattached, to the realities that bring pain and sorrow to our lives. Life is an ever-flowing stream. Attempting to hold onto the stream of life or fixate on certain experiences as necessary for our happiness leads to bondage, sorrow, and rebirth. While new age and new spirituality philosophies see reincarnation through the eyes of Western optimism as the opportunity for new experiences and lessons that will deepen our spiritual growth, still the wheel of birth continues until we discover the unity of our divine self with all other selves.

The doctrine of reincarnation, like the doctrines of heaven and hell, raises questions in the quest to understand the inequalities of life. On the one hand, the doctrine of heaven, with its focus on only one lifetime, has difficulty explaining why we are born with certain possibilities and limitations. Moreover, many people are so concerned with heaven that they forget that this is God's world, too. Further, the everlasting agony of hell far outweighs any human sinfulness. In the case of reincarnation, very few humans remember their past lives and are oblivious to the lessons they need to learn in this lifetime. Despite a myriad of lifetimes behind us, we have to start over with each new birth. Reincarnation may also, like the doctrine of heaven, minimize challenging social injustice in this lifetime. If the soul is the only authentic reality, as Hindu understandings of reincarnation assert, then what happens to us in this lifetime has an aura of unreality and unimportance. Until recent years, reincarnation was used to promote the caste system. The only way a lower caste member or an "untouchable" could move forward in the next life was to be content with this lifetime, and not agitate for social or economic reform. In a similar way, oppressed groups within Christianity, contrary to the prophets and Jesus, were often encouraged to accept their situations as God's will, living obediently in this passing world, with the hope of eternal salvation in the afterlife.

To its credit, the Buddhist image of "bodhisattva," an enlightened being who postpones the blissful freedom of Nirvana to help liberate others, describes the authentic spirit of everlasting life. If everyone around us possesses a divine spark, soul, spirit, or eternal aspect, our calling is to promote justice, dignity, and wholeness so that persons can discover their divinity in this life and the next. An eternal soul, the image of God in humankind, deserves to be treated as holy and valuable in this lifetime and with great compassion as he or she faces the realities of death.

CHAPTER FIVE
DYING WELL

"The greatest of these is love." (1 Corinthians 13:13)

The great Buddhist spiritual teacher, Dalai Lama once noted that it is blessing to be born into loving arms and die in loving arms. He was echoing the best wisdom of the world's religious traditions. Jesus proclaimed that what we do for the least of these, we are doing for God, and Jesus' ministry was the embodiment of God's love for humankind. In his compassion for the sick and dying and willingness to become unclean himself to insure the healing of others, Jesus has been described, along with the Greek physician, Hippocrates, as one of the two founders of Western medicine.

The Dalai Lama and Jesus both recognize that our common humanity and mortality inspires compassion. We are, as plaque announced at the Paris College of Surgeons, the dying caring for the dying. Vulnerability is the nature of life. Despite the uniqueness of each person's life, no one truly lives or dies alone. The intricate interdependence of life reminds us that we shape each other's experiences, and are able to bring life-transforming comfort and care to our most vulnerable companions. We need each other and we need companions for our final journey.

Extravagant Mortality. Each morning as I begin my walk on one of Cape Cod's beaches, I proclaim "This is the day that God has made and I will rejoice and be glad in it." Some days, I am exuberant; other mornings as I begin my walk, I feel the weight of the world upon my shoulders. Still, these words remind me that despite the challenges I face, I am alive and in this moment, God is with me, providing everything I need to experience and share God's joy with others. If God is present everywhere, then we don't need to die to go to heaven or experience God's presence in our lives. Heaven is right where we are, and ready to be discovered in every life situation, including our pilgrimages on life's darkest valleys.

Facing our dying is ultimately about faithful and extravagant living. Recently, my son Matt, a cancer survivor, shared an article from the Huffington Post, "I am a Dad with Stage 4 Cancer." On his way home from a beach holiday, the blog's author Oren Miller discovered that throughout the vacation, he had been present in body but not in spirit.

> It was only on the drive back home that I had the epiphany. It was only on the drive back that I realized what I had been missing out on. It was only on the drive back that I realized I had been experiencing the biggest tragedy of human existence: I was having the time of my life, and I didn't even know it.
> That was a good day, since once you make that decision, man... You're in Heaven every single second of your life. And it went on and on, and things only got better, because I made a conscious decision one summer day, on the drive home from Bethany Beach, and was able to repeat that decision subconsciously from that moment on. It made the difference between a living Hell, where I was always behind, always unhappy, and always unfulfilled — always a step behind on my writing, my relationship with my wife, with my friends, and with my kids, and a living Heaven, where even if I had wanted more out of life, I also knew I had it all.

A few years later, Oren Miller was diagnosed with an incurable cancer. Three months before his death, Oren Miller posted the following comment:

> Should I complain, though? Should I cry out to the empty sky and say, "Why me?" Or should I feel that now, even now, especially now, a little confused, a little tired, and a little sad, I'm having the time of my life?
> Whatever happens to my body in the next few months is still relatively unknown. Here's what we do know, though: We know I'm the luckiest sonofab*tch who's ever walked this earth, and we know I will be loved until my last moment by people it has been my utmost privilege to know: by a wife I adore and two kids I'm in awe of every single moment.

Miller uses the term "lucky" to describe his life. Others would use the term "blessed" or "graced" by the wondrous beauty of our mortal, finite, and imperfect lives. We are blessed because we are mortal and will someday say "goodbye" to everything and everyone we've loved on this good earth. Even if heaven is our destination, this is the day that God has made and we will rejoice and be glad in it. Mortality is a blessing. Because we don't have forever we can cherish this day and out of our gratitude for this day, we can say "yes" to becoming God's companions in bringing love and beauty to this good earth. This moment, the moment you are reading this book, is holy and unrepeatable. Rabbi Abraham Joshua Heschel described the wonder of each moment in terms of radical amazement:

> Our goal should be to live life in radical amazement.....
> get up in the morning and look at the world in a way that takes
> nothing for granted. Everything is phenomenal; everything
> is incredible; never treat life casually. To be spiritual is to be
> amazed.

There is an amazing grace to each moment, and in each moment we can find ourselves, rejoicing in our lives and loving with extravagance and joy.

Living While You're Dying. Life is amazing, but death is seldom easy. There are moments of despair, confusion, doubt, and pain. Our mortality can isolate us or it can drive us toward loving arms. It truly takes a village not only to raise a child, but to die with grace, dignity, and love. Last year, my mother-in-law Maxine Gould died at age 96. For virtually all of her 96 years, she was fiercely independent. As she aged, she struggled with letting go of tasks that had defined her life. But, after a urinary tract infection that led to pneumonia, she began to go downhill physically and mentally. We had just moved to Cape Cod, where I began my ministry at South Congregational Church in Centerville. We didn't have many friends, but within a few weeks the church rallied around the new pastor and his family. In the next six months, we received casseroles, freshly caught fish, smoked blue fish, and bottles of wine to soothe the spirit. Maxine received get well cards and friendship notes, some of which came from persons facing life-threatening illnesses themselves.

We realized that we couldn't do it alone. We were blessed to secure the services of caregivers through a local organization, Home

Instead. These caregivers provided companionship for Maxine, enabled my wife and I to go out to dinner, movies, and walks on the beach as well as go to work. They took care of her physical needs, engaged her in conversation, and cooked meals. I will never forget the loving presence of her caregivers. Maxine realized that she couldn't do it alone, and began to receive the loving acts of others with grace and gratitude.

Finally, the time came to call Hospice. I had recommended Hospice care to congregants and friends throughout my ministry, but now it was our turn to place Maxine's medical care in the hands of those who would enable her to die as she wished — at home, in comfort, and in the companionship of family.

Hospice reminded us that caregivers need care as well. If our wellsprings ran dry, we might not be able to give Maxine the love she needed in her final weeks. The grace of Hope Hospice and Home Instead enabled us to nurture ourselves and our relationship with confidence that Maxine was in good hands. Truly Maxine was blessed. She died at home, surrounded by Kate and me and nurtured by her familiar caregiver. She truly died in loving arms and was welcomed by the Loving Arms of Another, our Savior, whose love embraces all God's beloved children.

Despite our best efforts and deep love for friends and family, few deaths are easy. Helplessness and pain are often unendurable. Often medical interventions intended to help us make dying all the more painful and isolating. The challenges of dying in a technological society have inspired a growing interest in physician-assisted death, now legal in Oregon, Washington, and New Mexico, and more or less permitted in Montana. While I am not going into the question of assisted suicide or euthanasia in this text, it is clear to me that physician-assisted suicide is no more "playing God" than many of our current life-extending medical interventions. I believe that God has given us the freedom and creativity to choose our quality of life and to promote the well-being of our brothers and sisters. We don't need to endure unbearable suffering nor do we need to walk the way of the cross in imitation of Jesus. Jesus suffered so that we don't have to. God wants us to have abundant life even when death is imminent. God's love embraces us in every season of life. Nothing can separate us from the love of God, not even suicide or physician-aided death. Still, our quest is to welcome every child lovingly and to be loving midwives for others' final journey Home.

In the end, God's love casts out all fear and enables us to face what is beyond our control with the faith that God is with us and God has the final word for us and all creation, and that word is love. This faith is the inspiration to live and love fully from here to eternity.

TOPICAL LINE DRIVES

Straight to the Point in under 44 Pages

All Topical Line Drives volumes are priced at $5.99 print and $2.99 in all ebook formats.

Available

The Authorship of Hebrews: The Case for Paul	David Alan Black
What Protestants Need to Know about Roman Catholics	Robert LaRochelle
What Roman Catholics Need to Know about Protestants	Robert LaRochelle
Forgiveness: Finding Freedom from Your Past	Harvey Brown, Jr.
Process Theology: Embracing Adventure with God	Bruce Epperly
Holistic Spirituality: Life Transforming Wisdom from the Letter of James	
	Bruce Epperly
To Date or Not to Date: What the Bible Says about Pre-Marital Relationships	
	D. Kevin Brown
The Eucharist: Encounters with Jesus at the Table	Robert D. Cornwall
The Authority of Scripture in a Postmodern Age: Some Help from Karl Barth	
	Robert D. Cornwall
Pathways to Prayer	David Moffett-Moore
Rendering unto Caesar	Chris Surber
The Caregiver's Beattitudes	Robert Martin
What is Wrong with Social Justice	Elgin Hushbeck, Jr.
I'm Right and You're Wrong	Steve Kindle
Words of Woe: Alternative Lectionary Texts	Robert D. Cornwall
Stewardship: God's Way of Recreating the World	Steve Kindle
Why Christians Should Care about Their Jewish Roots	Nancy Petrey
Why Christians Should Care about Their Jewish Roots	Nancy Petrey

Forthcoming

God the Creator: The Variety of Christian Views on Origins	Henry Neufeld
A Cup of Cold Water	Chris Surber
Textual Criticism	Thomas Hudgins

Planned

Christian Existentialism	David Moffett-Moore

(The titles of planned volumes may change before release.)

Generous Quantity Discounts Available
Dealer Inquiries Welcome
Energion Publications — P.O. Box 841
Gonzalez, FL 32560
Website: http://energionpubs.com
Phone: (850) 525-3916

Also by Bruce Epperly

Wise, honest, and liberating.

Patricia Adams Farmer
Author of *Embracing a Beautiful God*

Also in the Topical Line Drives Series

This one hits it out of the park.

David Alan Black
Dave Black Online
http://daveblackonline.com/blog.htm

MORE FROM ENERGION PUBLICATIONS

Personal Study

Finding My Way in Christianity	Herold Weiss	$16.99
The Jesus Paradigm	David Alan Black	$17.99
When People Speak for God	Henry Neufeld	$17.99

Christian Living

Faith in the Public Square	Robert D. Cornwall	$16.99
Grief: Finding the Candle of Light	Jody Neufeld	$8.99
Crossing the Street	Robert LaRochelle	$16.99

Bible Study

Learning and Living Scripture	Lentz/Neufeld	$12.99
From Inspiration to Understanding	Edward W. H. Vick	$24.99
Luke: A Participatory Study Guide	Geoffrey Lentz	$8.99
Philippians: A Participatory Study Guide	Bruce Epperly	$9.99
Ephesians: A Participatory Study Guide	Robert D. Cornwall	$9.99
Evidence for the Bible	Elgin Hushbeck, Jr.	$16.99
When People Speak for God	Henry Neufeld	$17.99
Meditations on According to John	Herold Weiss	$14.99

Theology

Creation in Scripture	Herold Weiss	$12.99
Creation: the Christian Doctrine	Edward W. H. Vick	$12.99
Ultimate Allegiance	Robert D. Cornwall	$9.99
History and Christian Faith	Edward W. H. Vick	$9.99
The Journey to the Undiscovered Country	William Powell Tuck	$9.99
Philosophy for Believers	Edward W. H. Vick	$14.99

Ministry

Clergy Table Talk	Kent Ira Groff	$9.99
So Much Older Then ...	Robert LaRochelle	$9.99
Wind and Whirlwind	David Moffett-Moore	$9.99

Generous Quantity Discounts Available
Dealer Inquiries Welcome
Energion Publications — P.O. Box 841
Gonzalez, FL 32560
Website: http://energionpubs.com
Phone: (850) 525-3916

9 781631 992261